EYE SPY OUR WORLD

A LOOK-AND-FIND ACTIVITY BOOK

Pippa Chorley

Illustrations by
David Liew

Marshall Cavendish
Children

Eye Spy Our World
ISBN 978 981 5009 13 2

© 2022 Philippa McAlpine and David Liew

First published 2022
Reprinted 2023

Published by Marshall Cavendish Children
An imprint of Marshall Cavendish International

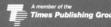
A member of the
Times Publishing Group

Other Marshall Cavendish Offices:
Marshall Cavendish Corporation, 800 Westchester Ave, Suite N-641, Rye
Brook, NY 10573, USA • Marshall Cavendish International (Thailand) Co Ltd,
253 Asoke, 16th Flr, Sukhumvit 21 Road, Klongtoey Nua, Wattana, Bangkok
10110, Thailand • Marshall Cavendish (Malaysia) Sdn Bhd, Times Subang,
Lot 46, Subang Hi-Tech Industrial Park, Batu Tiga, 40000 Shah Alam,
Selangor Darul Ehsan, Malaysia

Marshall Cavendish is a registered trademark of Times Publishing Limited

Printed in Singapore

Contents

Want to Play Eye Spy?

Kamal

Ling

Hello! My name is Ling and this is my friend Kamal. We love playing games and our favourite game is Eye Spy. Would you like to play too?

We are on a mission to discover amazing animals and plants from all around the world, and we'd love your help.

But keep an eye out for the evil Count Debris! He has been dumping rubbish, cutting down trees, spilling chemicals and stealing precious freshwater all over Planet Earth. If you spot him, let us know, so we can stop him and tell him about the dangers of destroying Earth's natural habitats.

Count Debris

Jasper

Don't forget to look out for my dog Jasper too! He loves to go exploring with us.

Thanks for helping us keep our planet green!

5

2 manatees

8 dragonflies

1 cottonmouth snake

9 ghost orchid plants

5 roseate spoonbills

3 alligators

Wetlands

Did you know that wetlands are areas of land covered by water? Sometimes the water is salty, sometimes fresh, and sometimes in-between.

Animals use wetlands for breeding and raising their young. Wetlands help filter and clean water, making it safe for people to use too. Without wetlands, places would be more at risk of storms and floods.

Sadly, wetlands are disappearing. They are drained to make space for farming or housing, polluted by fertilisers, or destroyed by the building of dams and factories.

We have come to the Everglades in Florida, USA, where Count Debris has been draining the water to build a gigantic factory. Can you find him and stop him before he ruins the wetlands?

7 large egrets

10 apple snails

6 redbelly turtles

4 minks

Polar Regions

Did you know that the polar regions cover the top and bottom of Planet Earth? The northern polar region is called the Arctic, and the southern polar region is called the Antarctic.

Polar regions store huge amounts of freshwater and help to regulate the temperature of the seas.

Sadly, due to climate change, the Arctic is getting warmer. Sea ice is shrinking, permafrost is melting, and coastlines are eroding. Animals such as polar bears and walruses are losing their habitats.

We have to stop Count Debris burning fossil fuels in his factories which contributes to climate change! Can you help us find him?

 3 Arctic foxes

9 Arctic cod

 4 polar bears

 8 Arctic hares

 5 walruses

1 narwhal   10 puffins   6 seals   2 orcas   7 lemmings

6 lions 10 termites 1 rhinoceros 7 zebras 2 leopards

Grasslands

Did you know that grasslands are large flat areas of land covered in grass? They are not as dry as a desert, but not as wet as a forest.

Grasslands are home to lots of grazing animals that live in herds, as well as their predators.

Sadly, most grasslands have been turned into fields of crops because they are the world's easiest places to farm. This leaves many grassland species endangered.

We have come to the East African savannah, as we heard that Count Debris is planning to build industrial farms here. Can you help us find all the animals and get them to an animal sanctuary where they can be protected?

8 acacia trees   5 hyenas   9 vultures   4 elephants   3 giraffes

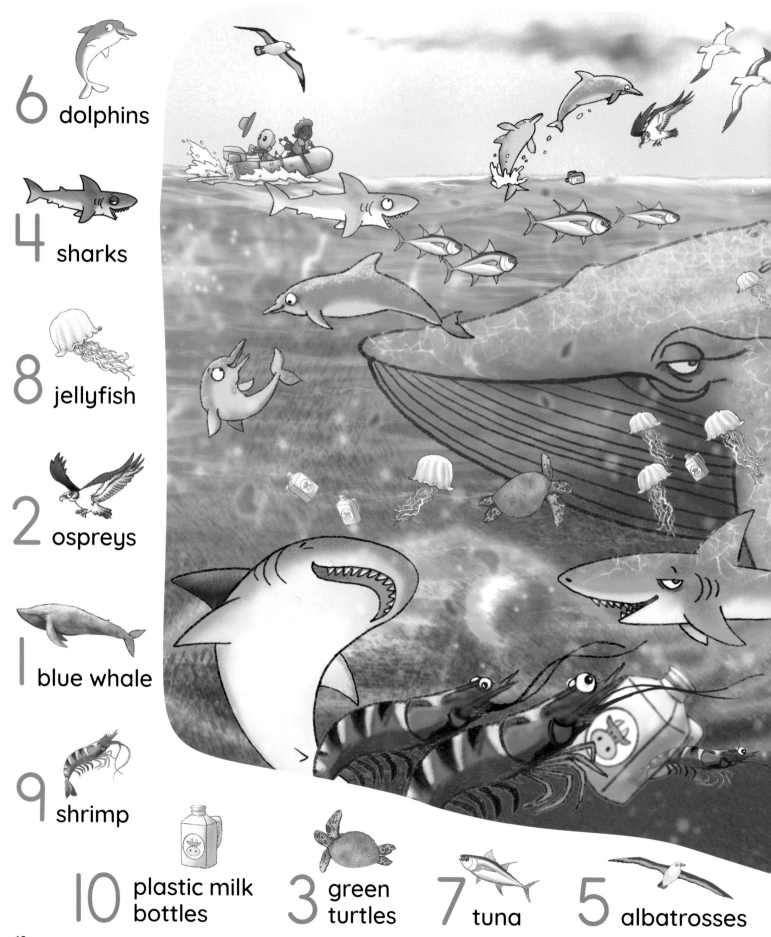

6 dolphins

4 sharks

8 jellyfish

2 ospreys

1 blue whale

9 shrimp

10 plastic milk bottles

3 green turtles

7 tuna

5 albatrosses

Oceans

Did you know that the ocean covers more than 70 per cent of the Earth's surface? There are five major ocean areas — the Pacific, Atlantic, Indian, Arctic and Southern.

This huge body of saltwater contains the greatest diversity of life on Earth, and billions of humans rely on it for fishing.

Sadly, because of overfishing and pollution, many ocean species are on the brink of extinction. In the Pacific Ocean, so much garbage has accumulated that it has created the Great Pacific Garbage Patch which is three times the size of France!

Can you help us find all the rubbish that Count Debris has dumped into the ocean so we can take it away to be recycled?

6 wild onions

9 jerboas

7 gerbils

1 gobi bear

4 bactrian camels

2 golden eagles

10 saxaul trees

3 wild horses

5 scorpions

Deserts

Did you know that deserts are barren areas with very little rainfall? Most are hot in the daytime and cold at night.

Animals and plants living in these harsh environments have special features to help them survive. Camels have humps that store fat for food, and cacti have stems that can store water.

Sadly, as human populations grow, they are moving into desert areas to farm crops and build houses. They draw precious groundwater and deprive native species of their source of water.

We have come to the Gobi Desert in Central Asia where Count Debris has been sucking up water to build a giant water park. Can you help us find him and stop him?

8 gazelles

6 Pacific salmon

8 flying squirrels

2 grizzly bears

3 moose

1 bald eagle

7 porcupines

5 wolves

10 mushrooms

4 beavers

Temperate Forests

Did you know that there are different types of forests? Temperate, tropical and boreal. Temperate forests never get too hot or too cold, and are home to many types of plants.

Temperate forests provide us with timber and oxygen. As trees grow, they remove harmful gases from our atmosphere and help make our air clean.

Sadly, forests are being destroyed for farming, mining, logging and construction. Deforestation threatens wildlife and destroys trees that take centuries to grow.

We have come to the largest temperate forest in Alaska, USA, where Count Debris has been chopping down trees to build a highway. Can you help us find him and stop him?

9 red cedar trees

Mountains

Did you know that mountains are home to some of the world's most extraordinary species, such as mountain gorillas and giant pandas? Mountains also store much needed freshwater as snow and ice, that keep rivers flowing throughout the year.

Sadly, mountains are being damaged by logging, which can lead to avalanches and landslides. Waste chemicals from factories also spill into mountain rivers, polluting the freshwater.

We have come to Mount Everest in the Himalayas, the highest mountain in the world. Count Debris has been dumping dangerous chemicals from his factories here. Can you help us find these chemicals before the snow melts and they pollute the rivers?

8 geese

5 yaks

10 prayer flags

7 rhododendron flowers

| snow leopard

9 pikas

18

3 wild donkeys

4 red foxes

2 red pandas

6 Himalayan monals

10 drinks cans   8 water hyacinths   6 sacred ibis   9 palm trees   2 Egyptian cobras

Freshwater Habitats

Did you know that rivers, creeks, lakes, ponds, swamps and marshes are all freshwater habitats?

Freshwater makes up less than 3 per cent of the world's water, but it supports more than 100,000 species, including humans.

Sadly, due to pollution and climate change, freshwater habitats are now endangered.

We have come to the famous Nile River in Africa. It is one of the longest rivers in the world. Most of Egypt depends on water from the Nile River to survive. Can you help us keep it clean and find the rubbish dumped by Count Debris?

 5 Nile crocodiles

 1 Nile perch

 4 baboons

 7 hippos

 3 feluccas

Coral Reefs

Aren't coral reefs pretty? Did you know that they are made up of thousands of tiny animals called polyps?

One-quarter of all known marine life depends on coral reefs for survival. Coral reefs also protect coastlines from storms. But they are very delicate and can be easily damaged by boats and pollution.

Plastic rubbish creates one of the worst problems for marine life. Plastics that float in the ocean break down into tiny pieces under the sun's heat. Polyps and other marine animals can mistake these pieces for food and swallow them.

Can you help us clear up the rubbish dumped by Count Debris in the Great Barrier Reef in Australia before it hurts any of the animals?

3 manta rays

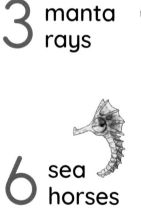
6 sea horses

5 fan coral

8 plastic yokes

9 sea anemones

1 whale shark

2 giant clams 7 starfish 10 angel fish 4 clown fish

Tropical Rainforests

Tropical rainforests are warm and wet. Did you know they are home to more than half of Earth's land animal species?

Rainforests absorb carbon dioxide from the air and cool the atmosphere. They are also a source of oxygen and freshwater, and they provide us with important life-saving medicines.

Sadly, huge areas of rainforest are being destroyed every minute for farming.

We have come to the world's largest rainforest, the Amazon, in South America. Can you help us stop Count Debris cutting down trees?

10 bullet ants

3 sloths

7 howler monkeys

6 piranhas

8 macaws

5 capybaras

1 anaconda

2 jaguars

4 river dolphins

9 poison dart frogs

5 red squirrels
2 foxes
6 blue tits
3 robins
1 badger

26

10 bumble bees

Urban Garden Homes

As human populations grow, they build and build, taking over more and more wildlife habitats. Many animals have had to adapt to living in urban environments to survive. But did you know, we can help them thrive too?

We have come to visit our friends in England, where they have been working hard to help the local wildlife. Can you see the insect hotel they have made from used plastic bottles, and the birdbath made from old plant pots? Maybe we can use some of Count Debris' rubbish that we have collected to do the same!

Can you spy Count Debris too? Let's show him all of the rubbish he has been dumping around the world and explain to him where and why it should be recycled!

7 ladybirds

4 hedgehogs

9 butterflies

8 earthworms

The Four Rs

Reduce, Reuse, Recycle and Renewable Energy

We have brought Count Debris to a recycling plant to show him all the things that can be recycled. Did you know even clothes and computers can be recycled?

Firstly, everything has to be sorted, separated and cleaned. Glass, metal and plastic are melted down and turned into new items. Paper is mixed together, washed and rolled out into cardboard.

This recycling plant is extra special as it is powered by clean, renewable energy, rather than fossil fuels. Solar panels collect sunlight, which generates electricity and heat. Wind turbines with giant blades spin as the wind blows. They convert wind energy to electrical energy through a machine called a generator. It's so amazing that even Count Debris is impressed. Let's hope he will be a planet protector and not a planet destroyer from now on!

6 newspapers

REUSE RECYCLE RENEW

GLASS... WHERE? ↓ HERE! ☺

ALUMINIUM

PLASTICS

FRAGILE!

PAPER

NEWS

ELECTRONICS

28

9 aluminium cans

8 plastic bottles

10 recycling symbols

3 egg cartons

4 solar panels

7 glass jars

1 recycling truck

5 mobile phones

2 wind turbines

RECYCLING CENTRE

NEWS

NEWS

How Can We Help?

We live in a beautiful world full of unique habitats, but sadly, many of these environments are under threat as human populations grow and demand more space, energy, food and water.

As humans burn more fossil fuels, build more factories and cut down more trees, they not only pollute and destroy environments, they also release harmful gases into the atmosphere. These gases trap heat and cause the earth and oceans to warm, leading to climate change.

It is such a huge problem that it might feel overwhelming. But if everyone makes small changes, the impact will be big!

 So what can we do to help protect our world?

♻ Plant a tree! The more trees we have, the cleaner our air will be. Trees also provide shelter for animals!

♻ Reduce the amount of energy we consume. Turn off lights and unplug electronics when not in use.

♻ Reduce the amount of fossil fuels we use. Cycle or walk rather than ride in a car.

♻ Say no to single-use plastic, such as bags, straws and bottles! (Did you know that most plastic is also made from petroleum, a fossil fuel?)

♻ Recycle wherever possible.

♻ Conserve precious water by taking shorter showers. Use undrunk water for cleaning or watering plants instead of pouring it away.

♻ Protect our oceans by only buying responsibly-farmed seafood.

♻ Donate to organisations that conserve our environments and protect animals that live in them.

Thank You for Playing

We had so much fun exploring with you and visiting all of Planet Earth's fascinating habitats. Our favourite was the rainforest, what was yours?

Thanks for helping us clean up all the rubbish dumped by Count Debris. We're glad we managed to track him down and teach him about the importance of looking after our world! I hope now he remembers the four Rs!

We've learnt so much about different ways we can help our planet stay green. Did you like my list? Is there anything you would add to it?

It's time for us to go home now. I can't wait to plant some flowers on my balcony for the bees and butterflies.

Thanks for helping us keep our world clean and green.

Come back and play again soon!

About the Author and Illustrator

Pippa Chorley is the awarding-winning author of *Counting Sheep, Stuffed!, Out of the Box* and *Eye Spy Singapore*. She grew up in a picturesque village in England, but soon found that the world was calling and set off to explore its many wonders and natural habitats.

Trained as a primary school teacher, Pippa loves to write stories for children that teach them about the world they live in and take them on their own adventures into imaginary worlds. She now lives in sunny Singapore with her husband, their three children and springer spaniel called Jasper.

David Liew has been drawing since he was able to hold a pencil. As an illustrator, David has worked on many children's storybook series, including the *Plano Adventures, Ellie Belly* and the *Adventures of Squirky the Alien*. His most recent work is a non-fiction illustrated series, *Change Makers*, with author, Hwee Goh.

When David is not creating worlds with his art, he is building them in the form of miniature landscapes and tabletop displays. He is the Regional Advisor for the Society of Children's Book Writers and Illustrators (SCBWI) in Singapore.